Isabella's Day at School

Meet the Feelings Family™

Childhood is a time of wonder, growth, and lots of feelings! Learning how to identify, express, and understand these feelings is an important part of social-emotional development.

At hand2mind, we believe that children learn best through play. This is why we created the Feelings Family, a relatable cast of characters who look and act like the feelings they represent. *Isabella's Day at School* follows Isabella and her friends through everyday adventures that evoke five core feelings familiar to young children. The Feelings Family characters appear in Isabella's imagination throughout the story to illustrate how feelings can **look** on the outside and **feel** on the inside— reflecting the five friendly plush toys in the set.

As you read the story, encourage children to play along and act out scenes with their plush toys. Take time to ask children what they notice and guide them to relate the toys, pictures, and story to their personal experiences. As each feeling is introduced in the story, ask children these questions to prompt and guide discussion:

- How can you tell what the character is feeling?

- How do you know when you feel this way?

- What do you do when you feel this way?

Extension activities are provided at the end of the book to help children dive deeper and learn to manage their feelings.

Let's get started!

This is a story about Isabella and her friends. They have lots of different feelings! When they feel a certain way, they do many different things.

Theo shakes when he is scared.

Aditi stomps when she is angry.

Isabella jumps when she is surprised.

Feelings come from inside us. Feelings can change, from happy to sad to angry—all in the same day!

One sunny morning, Isabella woke up and looked around her room.

She saw her favorite sweater on her chair.
She saw her picture hanging on the wall.
She pushed her toy truck across the floor.

It was Wednesday. And Wednesday meant waffles for breakfast. Isabella **loves** waffles!

Isabella feels happy.

Our eyes may sparkle when we are happy.

Our mouth could turn into a smile.

Being happy feels bright and bubbly.
We may want to laugh, dance, or **sing!**

"Thank you, Papa!" Isabella said between yummy, waffly bites.

Crunch! Crunch!

After breakfast, she walked to school with her best friend, Theo.

They were pretending to be dinosaurs (actually, Isabella was being a dinosaur ballerina) when—

Isabella and Theo heard a low buzzing sound coming from their neighbor's garden. When Isabella spotted the bee, she smiled.

But Theo froze when he saw it. He was shaking.

"Bees are wonderful!" Isabella said.

She stopped to watch the bee as it circled around and buzzed in the distance.

But Theo had stopped looking. His eyes were shut tight.

"Remember when we learned that bees help more flowers grow?" Isabella asked. "We need to let them do their work."

Theo pushed up his glasses and took a deep, deep breath.

"Let's watch from here together!" said Isabella.
The bee got closer to the flower and landed on it.

Theo watched the busy bee take a long sip from the flower, then fly off to find another one. "That's pretty cool," he thought.

At school, Isabella and Theo did a zillion fun things together.

They read incredible books...

They built tall, tall towers...

...and made funny masks.

97, 98, 99...

They even counted to A HUNDRED.

Isabella and Theo were painting when their friend Aditi stomped over.

"What's wrong, Aditi?" Theo asked.

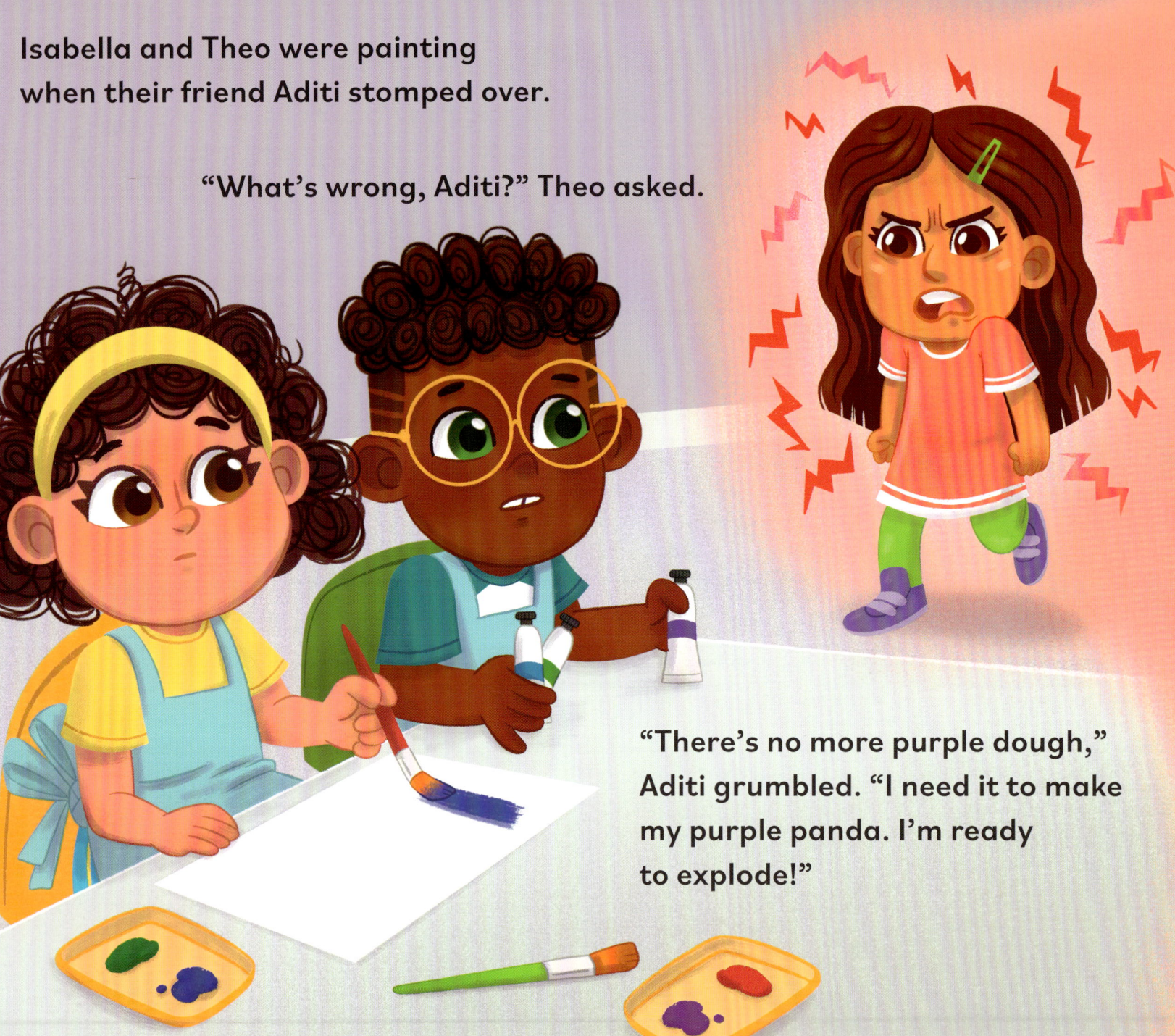

"There's no more purple dough," Aditi grumbled. "I need it to make my purple panda. I'm ready to explode!"

Aditi frowned and crossed her arms.

Theo had an idea to help his friend. "Would you like to paint with us instead?"

"We have purple paint!" Isabella called out.

Aditi thought about it, then nodded. "Okay. That could be fun."

It was Science time next. Isabella's teacher said they will build a volcano! Isabella had never seen a real volcano. She skipped around a bit, then put on her goggles and gloves to begin.

Isabella mixed and stirred, wondering what would happen.

Suddenly, **POW!** Foam fizzled and spouted and bubbled up...just like a volcano!

Isabella jumped back and yelped. **Yeee!** Inside, she felt like a burst of confetti.

Theo saw that Isabella was surprised. When he saw her experiment, he grinned. "Wow—can I make one?"

Isabella nodded with a chuckle, then showed Theo where the goggles and gloves were.

"Surprises can be fun sometimes," she thought.

Ding! Ding!

It was time to go outside.
Isabella and Theo waited at the door.

"Ready?" asked Theo.

"Ready!" said Isabella.

Isabella and Theo ran across the grass.
They headed straight for the playground swings.

"Isabella, look." Theo sighed, pointing to the swings.

"**NOOOO!**" Isabella wailed.

The swings were already taken.

Isabella and Theo are feeling sad.

We may want to cry or be alone when we are sad.

Sometimes we **sigh** or feel heavy inside.

We might huddle up in a cozy spot with something we love.

Isabella and Theo **slumped** side by side on a bench.

"Want to do something else?" offered Theo.

"Like what?" Isabella sighed. "Nothing sounds fun."

"Sometimes when I'm sad," Theo said, "I do a silly dance."

"A what dance?" Isabella frowned.

"A silly dance—you dance as silly as you can for five seconds," Theo explained.

"Okay," Isabella shrugged. "Show me."

Theo **whirled** and **wiggled**. He **hopped** and **bopped**.

Isabella wasn't sure what Theo was doing. But she decided to try it!

Isabella **jiggled** and **jumped**. She **twirled** and **twisted**.

"I feel a lot better," Isabella giggled.

"Me too," Theo grinned.
"Want to go down the slide?"

"YEAH!" Isabella cheered.

Isabella and Theo **zoomed** down the super tall, super loopy slide. **WEEE!**

"Theo, look." Isabella pointed. "The swings are open!"

Flying through the air with her best friend,
Isabella watched the other kids on the playground.

She saw feelings **EVERYWHERE**.

Which feelings do YOU see?

33

Talk About It

Extend discussion with the prompts below as you read the story.

Think of a time when you felt happy. **What did you do?** *(p. 6)*

Can you guess how Theo is feeling? *(p. 10)* **What do you notice about his face and body?**

Think of a time when you were scared. **How did you feel inside?** *(p. 11)*

Why do you think Theo took a deep breath? *(p. 12) **Try it! How do you feel?**

Why do you think Aditi is stomping? *(p. 16)* **What makes you feel this way?**

Have you ever helped a friend who was angry? *(p. 18)* **What did you do?**

Describe how Isabella is feeling. *(p. 20)*
How do you know?

Share examples of surprises you like and surprises you don't like. *(p. 21)*

What tells you how Isabella is feeling? *(p. 24)*
Do you think Theo feels the same way?

How do you think being silly could help when you are feeling sad? *(p. 28)*

What I Can Do When I Am...

Happy
- Invite your plush toy to a moving, grooving dance-a-thon!
- Hug someone or something you love.
- Write a note to help a friend feel better.

Sad
- Take long sips of a warm and soothing drink.
- Allow yourself to cry or just be quiet if you need to.
- Talk to a trusted adult or to your plush toy about how you feel.

Surprised
- Breathe in, then out, until your breathing slows down.
- Wiggle all your fingers and wiggle all your toes. Then, shake your plush toy!
- Take a break. Then, go back to what surprised you.

Scared
- Breathe in something that smells nice, like a flower or a warm cookie.
- Ask an adult to tell you about a time they were scared.
- Check your five senses! What do you see, hear, smell, taste, and touch right now?

Angry
- Scribble out your angry feelings all over a big piece of paper. Front and back!
- Find a quiet space and let out a big **ROAR**.
- Tighten your whole body. Then, let it all go.